Nico's List

Julia Wall
Heath McKenzie

 Nelson Thornes

Nelson Thornes

First published in 2007 by Cengage Learning Australia
www.cengage.com.au

This edition published under the imprint of Nelson Thornes Ltd,
Delta Place, 27 Bath Road, Cheltenham, United Kingdom, GL53 7TH

10 9 8 7 6 5 4 3 2
11 10 09 08

Nico's List
ISBN 978-1-4085-0159-7

Story by Julia Wall
Illustrations by Heath McKenzie
Edited by Cameron Macintosh
Designed by Karen Mayo
Series Design by James Lowe
Production Controller Seona Galbally
Audio recordings by Juliet Hill, Picture Start
Spoken by Matthew King and Abbe Holmes
Printed in China by 1010 Printing International Ltd

Website www.nelsonthornes.com

Nico's List

Julia Wall
Heath McKenzie

Contents

Chapter 1

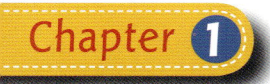

The Tickets

"Why are you cutting your toenails in here!" Maria yelled at me in the living room. "That is so gross!"

Then she slammed the door and stomped off to her room.

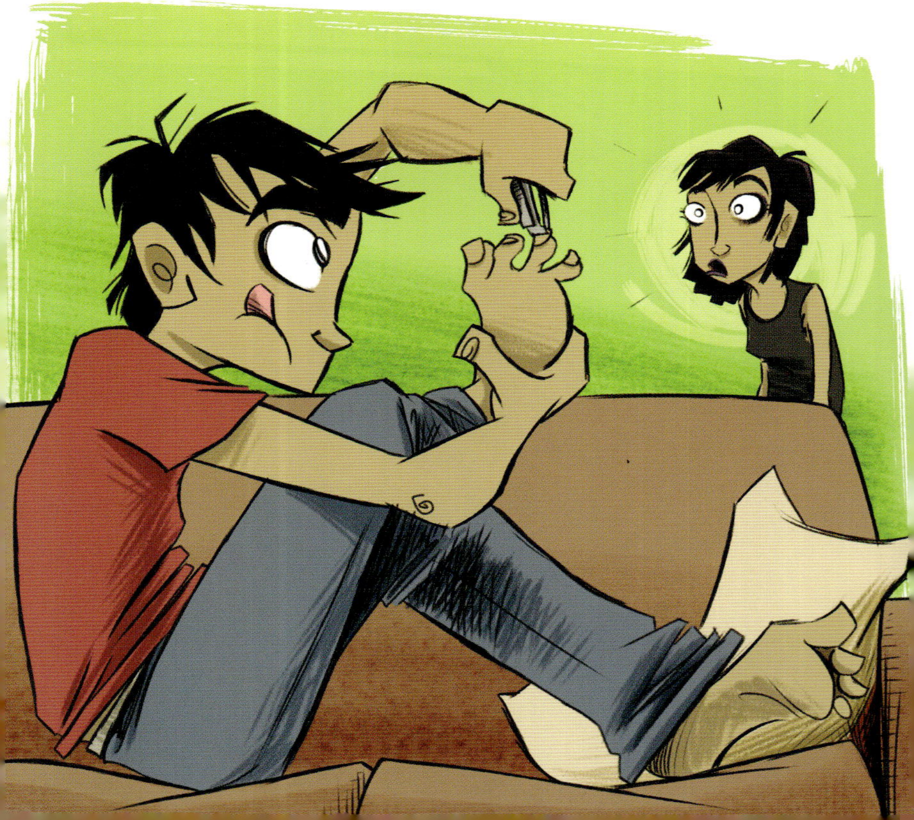

I knew why my sister was in
such a bad mood.
Her favourite band, the Sci-fi Zombies,
were coming to town
and she didn't have tickets.

I turned on the radio.
They were playing
a Sci-fi Zombies song.
It was one of Maria's favourites.
Luckily for me, it was the end
of the song.
"Great news, everyone,"
the announcer was saying.
"Be the ninth caller through
and win a double pass to see
the Sci-fi Zombies live in concert
this Friday!"

Suddenly, I had an idea.
I picked up the phone
and entered the station number
into speed dial.

A few minutes later,
I knocked on Maria's door.
She was lying on her bed,
mooning over a poster of Johnny Alien,
the lead singer of the Sci-fi Zombies.

"Hey, Maria," I said. "Guess what?"

"Go away," she scowled,
and turned on her side.

"I just called Radio Rad," I said,
"and won a double pass
to the Sci-fi Zombies concert."

Maria turned around.
"You did not," she said.

"I did too. They're sending me
the tickets today," I replied.

"But you don't even like them!"
she said.

"No," I said, "but you do,
so if you're my slave until Friday,
I'll give you the tickets."

"What do I have to do?" asked Maria.

I knew she'd give anything
to see Johnny Alien live.
"There are my jobs for a start," I said.
"This week I'm on kitchen stuff."

"I can do that," said Maria quickly.
"What else?"

Cool, I thought.
This was going to be a piece of cake.
"I don't know yet," I said.
"I'll let you know."

Chapter 2

The List

That night, Maria did my chores
while I put my feet up
and watched TV.
It was great.

The next morning, I asked Maria
for a lift to school.
We go to different schools,
and normally I take the bus.

"I'll be late!" she said.

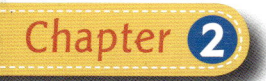

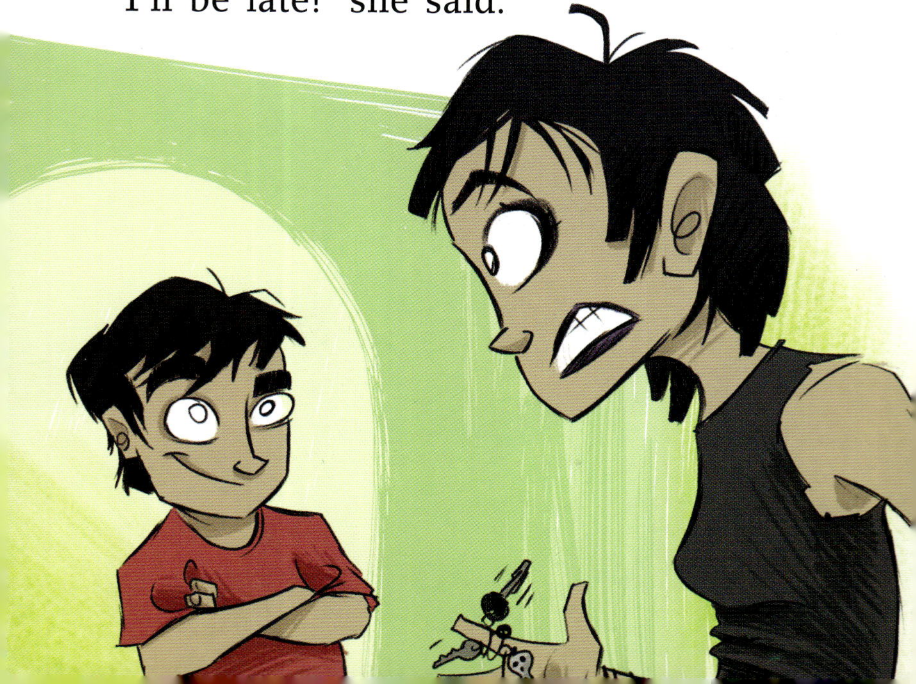

The Sci-fi Zombies tickets
had already arrived by courier.
I pulled them out of my pocket.
"Not if we leave now," I said.
"And remember, you have to be
my slave if you want to see
your beloved!"
I waved the tickets in front of her.

"Johnny Alien is not my beloved!"
But Maria turned red and picked up
her car keys.

It was great going to school
in Maria's car, instead of by bus.
By the time I got to school,
I'd thought of more things
that Maria could do before Friday.

I made a list.

1. Clean my football boots.
2. Wash my football kit.
3. Drop me off at the gym.
4. Help me with my homework.
5. Do anything else that I think of between now and Friday.

That night, I showed Maria the list.

"This had better be a good concert," she said.
Then she went and got my football boots from the hallway. "Oh, gross, Nico!" she said, looking at all the dried-on mud. "When was the last time you cleaned them?"

For the next two days,
my life was awesome.
Maria did everything on the list,
which meant I got time
to put my feet up.

Chapter 3

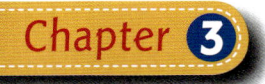

Cancelled!

On Thursday night,
Maria knocked on my door.
"What is it, slave?" I asked jokingly.

"I'm no longer your slave," said Maria.
"The concert's been cancelled.
I just heard it on the radio."
Then she ran back to her room.

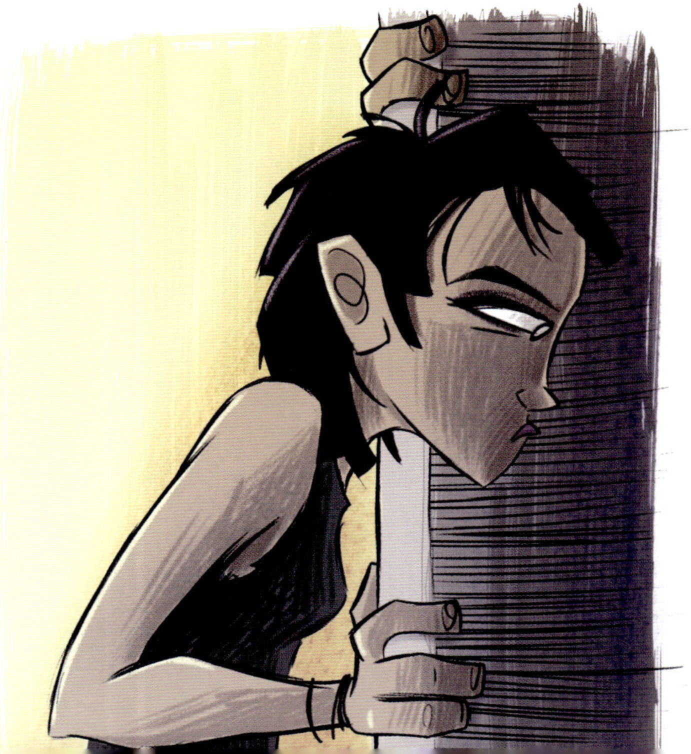

Oh well, I thought,
it was good while it lasted.
I decided to go and thank Maria
for all the stuff she'd done.

She was face down on her bed,
and I could tell she was crying.
"What is it?" she asked.

"I came to say thanks," I said,
"for helping me with my homework
and all the other stuff.
I'm sorry about the concert."

"Yeah, right."
Maria turned away from me.

I went back to my room,
and the phone rang.
It was Radio Rad,
saying sorry about the tickets
and offering me
something else instead.
I knew exactly what I was going to do
with what they gave me.

Chapter 4

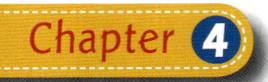

The CD

The next day, the courier was back.
"Hey, Maria," I said.
"I've got something for you."

"Go away," she said.
"I don't want to talk to you."

"Go on," I said. "Open it."

Maria looked at the parcel.
I could tell she was curious.

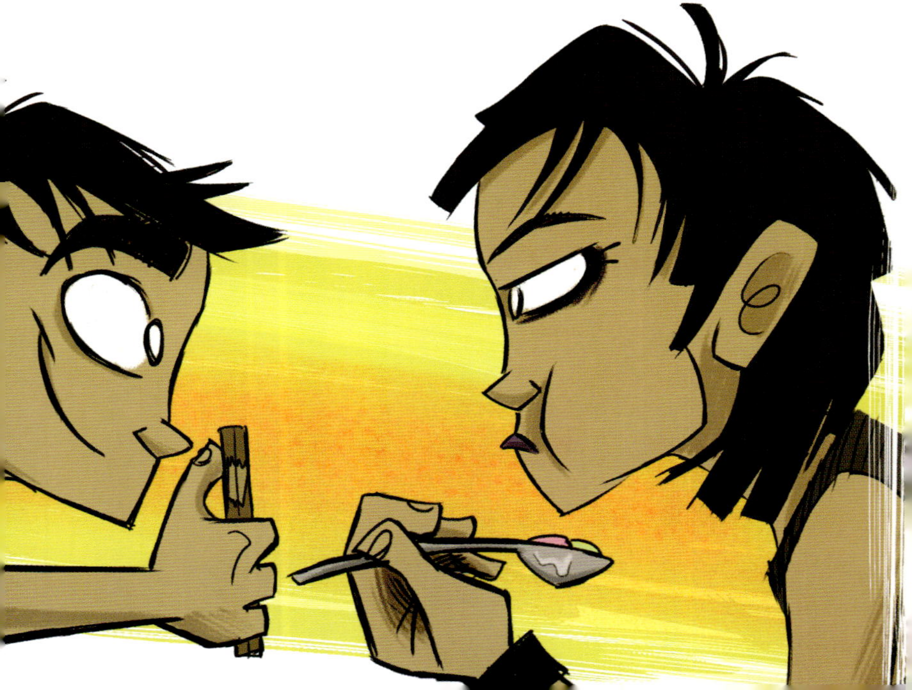

"Oh well," I said,
pretending to leave.
"If you don't want to listen to
the new Sci-fi Zombies double CD,
I'll listen to it myself."

'Mouse-traps' was the Sci-fi Zombies'
new CD.
I knew Maria was saving up for it.

Maria grabbed the parcel from me and ripped it open.

"Did you get this from Radio Rad?" she asked.

I nodded.

"I guess I'm just lucky," I said.

"Having you for a sister," I added.

"Oh, don't be such an idiot!" she said.

But I could tell she was over the moon.